The "Write" Way To Spell

Volume II

Workbook

by Marcia Weinstein, Ph.D.

BOOK LAB PUBLISHER PO BOX 230206 NEW YORK, NY 0023-0206

Published by:
Book Lab publishers
PO Box 230306
New York,NY 10023-0206
Voice 212 874-5534 . 800 644-4081
Fax 212 874-3105 . E Mail Booklabpub@aol.com

The "Write" Way To Spell, Vol. 2 workbook
Book # 2308 ISBN 87594-278-4
The "Write" Way To Spell, Vol. 2 Teacher's Guide
Book # 2309 ISBN 87594-279-2

The "Write" Way To Spell, Vol. 1 workbook
Book # 2304 ISBN 87594-216-4
The "Write" Way To Spell, Vol. 1 Teacher's Guide
Book # 2305 ISBN 87594-217-2

Printed in the United States of America. 2001

BOOK LAB

The "Write" Way To Spell

Volume II

Workbook

by Marcia Weinstein, Ph.D.

LESSON 1

A. SPELL YOUR NEW WORDS

1. ____________
2. ____________
3. ____________
4. ____________
5. ____________
6. ____________

B. FILL IN THE BLANKS WITH YOUR SPELLING WORDS

1. We saw two good ________ on TV last night.
2. Let's go to the ______ and fly kites after lunch.
3. There are lots of shops and a ________ theater at the new ______ in town.
4. Our ______ has a great library where I like to go on Saturday mornings.
5. We have to stop at the ________ for some bread and milk.

C. WHICH IS RIGHT?

want wants

wanting wanted

She________eggs for lunch but we have none.

What did he ________?

What do you think they will be ________ for lunch?

I________to go home early but I couldn't.

D. SENTENCE DICTATION

1. ____________
2. ____________
3. ____________
4. ____________
5. ____________
6. ____________
7. ____________
8. ____________
9. ____________
10. ____________

E. PROBLEM WORDS

1. ____________
2. ____________
3. ____________
4. ____________
5. ____________

F.

FILL IN THE BLANKS WITH YOUR SPELLING WORDS

We used to like going to the mall in our ________. We could get a hamburger or play a game. But it's not fun now. Some gangs hang out there. They dirty the grass in the little ________ and they mess with us kids. They bother us at the ________ theater. They knock down cans and boxes in the food ________ just to make trouble. I think the store owners at the ________ should do something about it. I have some good ideas about what they could do if they would ask me.

G.

MAKING SENTENCES

1. mall our town

1. ____

____

____

2. movies don't like

2. ____

____

H.

MY OWN WRITING

____

Describe a shopping mall in or near your town.

____

____

____

____

____

I.

WHICH ONE SHOULD YOU USE?

to too

1. I have to go ______ the market tomorrow.
2. If you go into town I want to go ______ .
3. "There's ______ much garbage at the mall," said Marla.
4. Let's go ______ the movies tonight.
5. Dad has ______ work late tonight.

HOW YOU DID

Spelling ________

	Super	Good	Getting Better	Needs Lots of Work
Punctuation				
Appearance				
Creativity				

LESSON 2

A. SPELL YOUR NEW WORDS

1. ______
2. ______
3. ______
4. ______
5. ______
6. ______
7. ______
8. ______

C. WHAT CONTRACTION COULD YOU USE INSTEAD

She is a pretty woman.

He is a smart boy.

I am all by myself today.

I will get that for you.

He will be fine if you leave him alone.

E. PROBLEM WORDS

1. ______
2. ______
3. ______
4. ______
5. ______

B. FILL IN THE BLANKS WITH YOUR SPELLING WORDS

1. Please ______ me look for my shoes.
2. We were ______ for you ______ night but we didn't see you.
3. He was ______ me make a movie for my project.
4. Let's go ______. We can buy something for lunch.
5. Can you ______ me how to ______ this new bike?

D. SENTENCE DICTATION

______

1. ______

______

2. ______

______

3. ______

______

4. ______

______

5. ______

______

6. ______

______

7. ______

______

8. ______

______

9. ______

______

10. ______

______

F.

FILL IN THE BLANKS WITH YOUR SPELLING WORDS

________ night I had to go ______________ with my brother. We wanted to ________ for something good to buy for dinner. So we took a ________ downtown. On the way we stopped at his friend's house. He wanted to ________ me a model ship they made together. It was so great I couldn't stop ___________ at it. I really love ships. Maybe he could ________ me make one too. That's all I could think of while I was ___________ him choose dinner.

G.

MAKING SENTENCES

1. last night show — 1. ______________________________

2. help do marketing — 2. ______________________________

H.

MY OWN WRITING

Write about a pet you have or would like to have.

I.

WHICH ONE SHOULD YOU USE?

when went

1. I don't know ________ we can go.
2. ________ can you ride into town with me?
3. We all ________ out for a pizza.
4. You must be done ________ the bell rings.
5. When we ________ to the park yesterday, it was raining.

HOW YOU DID

Spelling ________

	Super	Good	Getting Better	Needs Lots of Work
Punctuation				
Appearance				
Creativity				

LESSON 3

A. SPELL YOUR NEW WORDS

1. ______
2. ______
3. ______
4. ______
5. ______
6. ______
7. ______

B. FILL IN THE BLANKS WITH YOUR SPELLING WORDS

1. A gift from my brother ______ yesterday.
2. Do ______ from other lands ______ about our country?
3. My ______ wasn't in school last week and I missed him.
4. I think we should try to be ______ with everybody.
5. My ______ comes home from work very late.

C. PUT YOUR SPELLING WORDS IN ABC ORDER

1. ______
2. ______
3. ______
4. ______
5. ______
6. ______
7. ______

D. SENTENCE DICTATION

1. ______
2. ______
3. ______
4. ______
5. ______
6. ______
7. ______
8. ______
9. ______
10. ______

E. PROBLEM WORDS

1. ______
2. ______
3. ______
4. ______
5. ______

F. FILL IN THE BLANKS WITH YOUR SPELLING WORDS

Last month I ________ to live in the United States with my father. My mother and the rest of the __________ are still in Cuba. We are staying with some nice people until my __________ can make enough money to bring the whole family here. Everyone is very __________. I go to school and my _________, Miss Kelly, says she will help me ________ English first. Then she will ________ me many other things.

G. MAKING SENTENCES

1. children, school, learn

1. ______________________________

2. teacher, friendly, good

2. ______________________________

H. MY OWN WRITING

Describe your favorite teacher.

I. WHICH ONE SHOULD YOU USE?

teach learn

1. Let's see if we can ________ to play this game.
2. I think I can ________ if you ________ me slowly.
3. You will never ________ that bird to talk.
4. If somebody will ________ me, I know I can ________ to swim.
5. Will you ________ me to play the guitar?

HOW YOU DID

Spelling ________

	Super	Good	Getting Better	Needs Lots of Work
Punctuation				
Appearance				
Creativity				

LESSON 4

A. SPELL YOUR NEW WORDS

1. ____
2. ____
3. ____
4. ____
5. ____
6. ____
7. ____

B. FILL IN THE BLANKS WITH YOUR SPELLING WORDS

1. She was ____ her new kitten to the class.
2. Please don't bring your ____ car to school again.
3. My family lives in a small town near a big ____.
4. The city mouse and the ____ mouse are cousins.
5. I listened to the ____ game on my ____.

C. WHICH IS RIGHT?

help helps
helped helping

They ____
Bob cut his grass yesterday.

I won't be ____
you today.

Please ____ me.

She ____ me
with my homework every day.

D. SENTENCE DICTATION

1. ____
2. ____
3. ____
4. ____
5. ____
6. ____
7. ____
8. ____
9. ____
10. ____

E. PROBLEM WORDS

1. ____
2. ____
3. ____
4. ____
5. ____

F.

FILL IN THE BLANKS WITH YOUR SPELLING WORDS

My friend Tony lives on a farm in the __________. My family lives in a big__________. Last summer Tony came to stay with us. I started by____________him all of our__________. Then we went to the park to play__________. I took along a__________so we could listen to music. Tony said that our park is something like the country but there are too many tall buildings around it.

G.

MAKING SENTENCES

1. city / showing / friends

1. ____________________

2. country / from / what

2. ____________________

H.

MY OWN WRITING

Tell about a trip you took (to the city, country, or another town).

I.

WHICH ONE SHOULD YOU USE?

there their

1. Will you go over ________ with me?
2. Where are ________ friends today?
3. I don't know if ________ are any apples in ________.
4. Do you know where they put ________ games?
5. I don't like ________ house. It's too big.

HOW YOU DID

Spelling ________

Super	Good	Getting Better	Needs Lots of Work

Punctuation

Appearance

Creativity

LESSON 5

A. SPELL YOUR NEW WORDS

1. ____________
2. ____________
3. ____________
4. ____________
5. ____________
6. ____________

B. FILL IN THE BLANKS WITH YOUR SPELLING WORDS

1. We are ________ a math test ________.
2. The job was done very ________.
3. It ________ a long time to get home yesterday.
4. How ________ is it from your house to mine?
5. She was sitting ________ the teacher's desk.

C. PUT YOUR SPELLING WORDS IN ABC ORDER

1. ____________
2. ____________
3. ____________
4. ____________
5. ____________
6. ____________

D. SENTENCE DICTATION

1. ____________
2. ____________
3. ____________
4. ____________
5. ____________
6. ____________
7. ____________
8. ____________
9. ____________
10. ____________

E. PROBLEM WORDS

1. ____________
2. ____________
3. ____________
4. ____________
5. ____________

F. FILL IN THE BLANKS WITH YOUR SPELLING WORDS

My mother wasn't feeling very________ last night. So ________ my father ________ us out to my grandmother's house. She lives on a farm ________ out in the country. It's beautiful and I like it here, but I hope my Dad will be ________ us home soon because I want to be ________ my mother. And besides, I could be a big help to her.

G. MAKING SENTENCES

1. taking / father / far

1. ________

2. feel / well / today

2. ________

H. MY OWN WRITING

Tell about a time you helped someone.

I. WHICH ONE SHOULD YOU USE?

near nearer nearly nearby

1. Please come a little ________ to me.
2. She ________ got hit by a car, but it just missed her.
3. My friend, Julie lives ________.
4. Don't you come ________ me with those dirty hands.
5. It's ________ time to get ready to go.

HOW YOU DID

Spelling ________

	Super	Good	Getting Better	Needs Lots of Work
Punctuation				
Appearance				
Creativity				

LESSON 6

A. SPELL YOUR NEW WORDS

1. ____________
2. ____________
3. ____________
4. ____________
5. ____________
6. ____________
7. ____________

B. FILL IN THE BLANKS WITH YOUR SPELLING WORDS

1. These days most ________ and __________ have to work.
2. The little ________ in the blue dress is my sister.
3. In 1969 a ________ first walked on the moon.
4. The __________ took her new ________ to the doctor.
5. Which _______ made that great home run?

C. WHAT CONTRACTION COULD YOU USE INSTEAD

They are coming late this morning.

We are too late for the 10 o'clock show.

You are the tallest one here.

Let us take the baby home.

Don't you think **it is** time to go?

D. SENTENCE DICTATION

1. ____________
2. ____________
3. ____________
4. ____________
5. ____________
6. ____________
7. ____________
8. ____________
9. ____________
10. ____________

E. PROBLEM WORDS

1. ____________
2. ____________
3. ____________
4. ____________
5. ____________

F.

FILL IN THE BLANKS WITH YOUR SPELLING WORDS

One night I was watching a real horror show on TV. It was about how a big crack opened up in a street and all this slimy purple stuff came out of the ground and started to ooze all over the city. It oozed into a school and ate up every______ and ______ in the class. It ate up all the ______ and ______ who were going home from work. Soon it covered the whole city. One ______ and one ______ got away with their little ______ . It was a very silly show.

G.

MAKING SENTENCES

1. woman
baby
girl

1. ____________________

2. women
men
like

2. ____________________

H.

MY OWN WRITING

Tell about a time someone helped you.

I.

WHICH ONE SHOULD YOU USE?

man men woman women

1. Those three ______ in the black dresses are friends of mine.
2. See that ______ driving the truck? He knows my father.
3. There is a nice ______ at our market. She always smiles at me.
4. Some ______ and ______ in our neighborhood are planning a party.
5. Some of the teachers in my school are women, but many of them are ______ .

HOW YOU DID

Spelling ______

	Super	Good	Getting Better	Needs Lots of Work
Punctuation				
Appearance				
Creativity				

LESSON 7

A. SPELL YOUR NEW WORDS

1. ______
2. ______
3. ______
4. ______
5. ______
6. ______
7. ______

B. FILL IN THE BLANKS WITH YOUR SPELLING WORDS

1. It feels good to ______ a cold soda on a hot day.
2. Can you ______ a good ______ of a horse?
3. Watching the late movie made me feel very ______ .
4. Don't fall ______ before you finish studying.
5. I need eight hours of ______ to feel good in the morning.

C. WHICH IS RIGHT?

learn learns
learning learned

We ______ a lot last week.

We are ______ things all the time.

Let's ______ some more about space.

She ______ more every day.

D. SENTENCE DICTATION

______

1. ______
______
2. ______
______
3. ______
______
4. ______
______
5. ______
______
6. ______
______
7. ______
______
8. ______
______
9. ______
______
10. ______
______

E. PROBLEM WORDS

1. ______
2. ______
3. ______
4. ______
5. ______

F. FILL IN THE BLANKS WITH YOUR SPELLING WORDS

Sometimes I babysit for my mother's friend's baby. Most of the time I just have to give him a ________ of milk and put him to________. But last night he just wasn't________. He wouldn't ________ asleep. So I took him on my lap and read to him. Then I had this idea to________ a ________ of people sleeping. I showed it to him and sang him a song and soon he was fast ________.

G. MAKING SENTENCES

1. fall asleep can't

1. ____

2. picture draw sleepy

2. ____

H. MY OWN WRITING

What is something you would like to learn? Why would you like to learn it?

____

I.

WHICH ONE SHOULD YOU USE?

what want

1. I don't know ________ to do with myself today.
2. I ________ to go to town but I can't.
3. We all ________ to go marketing at the new mall.
4. ________ movie did you see last night?
5. Do you know ________ you will ________ to do after dinner?

HOW YOU DID

Spelling ________

	Super	Good	Getting Better	Needs Lots of Work
Punctuation				
Appearance				
Creativity				

LESSON 8

A. SPELL YOUR NEW WORDS

1. ____________
2. ____________
3. ____________
4. ____________
5. ____________
6. ____________
7. ____________

B. FILL IN THE BLANKS WITH YOUR SPELLING WORDS

1. We haven't had our car________ last summer.
2. The little boy tied the rope all by________ .
3. A ________ race was run by________ teams.
4. Please put that________airplane ________ in your desk.
5. She hurt ________ badly when she slipped on the ice.

C. WHICH IS RIGHT?

ask asks
asking asked

I'm only________
for help because I'm stuck.

They________ me
to their party last year.

Please don't ________
me that.

She ________ me
when she needs help.

D. SENTENCE DICTATION

1. ____________
2. ____________
3. ____________
4. ____________
5. ____________
6. ____________
7. ____________
8. ____________
9. ____________
10. ____________

E. PROBLEM WORDS

1. ____________
2. ____________
3. ____________
4. ____________
5. ____________

F.

FILL IN THE BLANKS WITH YOUR SPELLING WORDS

I have had a newspaper route ________ summer. It's hard work, but I want the money. I have to work________ to get to all the houses and ________ before dark. Some days the wind blows so hard a ________ might blow away. And some days I can't do the job by myself. I need ________ my brother and sister to help me. Then, if I'm sick, my sister might do it all by __________ or my brother might have to do it by __________ . Then I have to pay them for helping. But I still do OK.

G.

MAKING SENTENCES

1. fast, ride, both

1. ______________________________

2. since, back, came

2. ______________________________

H.

MY OWN WRITING

Tell about something important you did by yourself.

I.

WHICH ONE SHOULD YOU USE?

of   off

1. Which______these do you want to take home?
2. Please tell me when to get ______the bus.
3. I'm not taking______this coat. It's cold.
4. I'll take one______these and______ those.
5. Did you see that jet taking______?

HOW YOU DID

Spelling ________

	Super	Good	Getting Better	Needs Lots of Work
Punctuation				
Appearance				
Creativity				

LESSON 9

A. SPELL YOUR NEW WORDS

1. ______
2. ______
3. ______
4. ______
5. ______
6. ______
7. ______
8. ______

B. FILL IN THE BLANKS WITH YOUR SPELLING WORDS

1. It's too ______ to go to the movies ______.
2. It was much ______ than I thought it was.
3. ______ don't be ______ for my class play.
4. Have you been ______ to fix the radio?
5. ______ I ______ to catch a lightning bug in my hands.

C. WHICH CONTRACTION COULD YOU USE INSTEAD

They have gone to the store.

You have done all the work I asked you to do.

I have been the only one helping.

We have never gone alone.

I don't think **they have** finished yet.

D. SENTENCE DICTATION

______

1. ______
______
2. ______
______
3. ______
______
4. ______
______
5. ______
______
6. ______
______
7. ______
______
8. ______
______
9. ______
______
10. ______
______

E. PROBLEM WORDS

1. ______
2. ______
3. ______
4. ______
5. ______

F.

FILL IN THE BLANKS WITH YOUR SPELLING WORDS

I thought that when my little sister was born I would get to do more things because I was older. But when I ________ asking my mother if I might stay up a little ________ at night she said, "Not _____ , Bill. You go to sleep pretty ________ as it is and you have to get up so ________ for school."
So this week I tried ________ more. " ________ , Mom," I begged, "just a little later."
"Soon," she said. So I guess I'll just have to keep ________ .

G.

MAKING SENTENCES

1. tried / early / once

1. ______________________________

2. please / later / don't

2. ______________________________

H.

MY OWN WRITING

Tell about a time you got caught in a storm. If this never happened pretend that it did.

I.

WHICH ONE SHOULD YOU USE?

want won't

1. What do you ________ to do tonight?
2. I ________ go to school tomorrow if I don't feel better.
3. Why ________ you come with me?
4. I ________ do what you ________ if you don't do what I ask you.
5. Do you ________ any help with your school work tonight?

HOW YOU DID

Spelling ________

	Super	Good	Getting Better	Needs Lots of Work
Punctuation				
Appearance				
Creativity				

LESSON 10

A. SPELL YOUR NEW WORDS

1. ____________
2. ____________
3. ____________
4. ____________
5. ____________
6. ____________

C. WHICH IS RIGHT?

use uses using used

Shall we________this one?

I________every one already.

What are you________to fix that?

She________white paper to write her letters.

E. PROBLEM WORDS

1. ____________
2. ____________
3. ____________
4. ____________
5. ____________

B. FILL IN THE BLANKS WITH YOUR SPELLING WORDS

1. I felt so ________ when I lost the race.
2. This math test has ________ very ________ .
3. Of all the drinks here I like lemonade the ________ .
4. Which book will you read ________ .
5. Would you be ________to live here forever?

D. SENTENCE DICTATION

____

1. ____________

____

2. ____________

____

3. ____________

____

4. ____________

____

5. ____________

____

6. ____________

____

7. ____________

____

8. ____________

____

9. ____________

____

10. ____________

____

F.

FILL IN THE BLANKS WITH YOUR SPELLING WORDS

I think that ________ of the time I'm a pretty ________ person. I like a lot of things and my family is nice. But one thing has not ________ so great. My mother works very ________ and comes home late. I don't get to be with her much and it makes me ________ to see her so tired. But she says that ________ year she is going to try to get a job where she can work less. That should be much better.

G.

MAKING SENTENCES

1. happy, most, friends

1. ____________________

2. hard, unhappy, homework

2. ____________________

H.

MY OWN WRITING

Describe your favorite TV show.

I.

WHICH ONE SHOULD YOU USE?

no know

1. Don't you ________ that isn't his?
2. ________, I don't.
3. I need to ________ how much to get.
4. She asked if I ________ how to skate and I said ________.
5. ________, I don't think you have to ________ that.

HOW YOU DID

Spelling ________

	Super	Good	Getting Better	Needs Lots of Work
Punctuation				
Appearance				
Creativity				

LESSON 11

A. SPELL YOUR NEW WORDS

1. ____________
2. ____________
3. ____________
4. ____________
5. ____________
6. ____________

B. FILL IN THE BLANKS WITH YOUR SPELLING WORDS

1. Don't ________ to buy milk when you go to the store.
2. I think you and I should go ____________.
3. He had __________ to swim very well.
4. I _________ to clean my room this morning.
5. I am __________ as _______ as my brother Bill.

C. WHICH IS RIGHT?

see sees
seeing saw

How far can you _______ on a clear day?

I _________ an old friend this morning.

I wish we were ________ a movie.

She _________ her best friend every day.

D. SENTENCE DICTATION

1. ____________________
2. ____________________
3. ____________________
4. ____________________
5. ____________________
6. ____________________
7. ____________________
8. ____________________
9. ____________________
10. ____________________

E. PROBLEM WORDS

1. ____________
2. ____________
3. ____________
4. ____________
5. ____________

F.

FILL IN THE BLANKS WITH YOUR SPELLING WORDS

Some people don't forget what they ________. But I do. Mostly I have trouble learning to read. Whenever I learn something new I ________ some of the ________ stuff. Sometimes I think I ________ get a word or a sound in my head, but the next time I see it I know I ________ it already. Then I have to try to learn it all over again. I ________ have to work much harder than most people to learn other things. But I know I can, so I just keep at it until I get it.

G.

MAKING SENTENCES

1. almost / forgot / learned

1. ____

____

2. old / forget / also

2. ____

____

H.

MY OWN WRITING

____

Tell about once when you forgot something important.

____

____

____

____

I.

WHICH ONE SHOULD YOU USE?

to too two

1. Can I go ______?
2. Let's take ______ cookies each.
3. Will you please take this paper ______ your teacher
4. I need the ______ of you to go ______ the market for me.
5. First I want Joe to read. Then you can read ______.

HOW YOU DID

Spelling ________

	Super	Good	Getting Better	Needs Lots of Work
Punctuation				
Appearance				
Creativity				

LESSON 12

A. SPELL YOUR NEW WORDS

1. ______________
2. ______________
3. ______________
4. ______________
5. ______________
6. ______________

B. FILL IN THE BLANKS WITH YOUR SPELLING WORDS

1. My grandmother ________ us from the country today.
2. Yesterday I ______ too many hot dogs and felt sick.
3. The glass of milk is too ______ for the baby to ______.
4. Please stand up when I ______ your name.
5. Our family will ______ lunch at noon today.

C. WHICH IS RIGHT?

make makes
making made

She ________ me angry sometimes.

We are ________ cupcakes this afternoon.

I know he ________ you sad when he did that.

Don't ________ any more of those.

D. SENTENCE DICTATION

____

1. ______________________________

____

2. ______________________________

____

3. ______________________________

____

4. ______________________________

____

5. ______________________________

____

6. ______________________________

____

7. ______________________________

____

8. ______________________________

____

9. ______________________________

____

10. ______________________________

____

E. PROBLEM WORDS

1. ______________
2. ______________
3. ______________
4. ______________
5. ______________

F.

FILL IN THE BLANKS WITH YOUR SPELLING WORDS

I didn't feel too well last night. I got a phone ______ to come to baseball practice after dinner, so I asked my mom to make dinner early. But she ________ me in late and made so much to ______ that I thought I would never finish. So I ______ much too fast. There I was at the game having to ______ my belly because it was too ______ . It sure wasn't easy running with all that food in me.

G.

MAKING SENTENCES

1. ate, full, much

1. ______________________________

2. called, eat, friend

2. ______________________________

H.

MY OWN WRITING

Tell what happened when you came home late one day.

____

I.

WHICH ONE SHOULD YOU USE?

who how

1. Do you know ______ to play this game?
2. Do you know ______ that woman was?
3. ______ do you know what country they come from?
4. I can't tell ______ did that.
5. ______ knows that woman over there.

HOW YOU DID

Spelling ______

	Super	Good	Getting Better	Needs Lots of Work
Punctuation				
Appearance				
Creativity				

LESSON 13

A. SPELL YOUR NEW WORDS

1. ______________
2. ______________
3. ______________
4. ______________
5. ______________
6. ______________

B. FILL IN THE BLANKS WITH YOUR SPELLING WORDS

1. There is ________ left in the cookie jar.
2. Let's ________ the ________ out of the pool before we go swimming.
3. Did he ________ his leg when he fell?
4. I watched my sister ________ my mom was marketing.
5. You are so ________ you had better take a bath.

C. WHICH IS RIGHT?

come comes
coming came

My uncle ______ to dinner last week.

My sister ________ with me when I go shopping.

Will they be ________ with us?

Did she ______ to see the new puppy yet?

D. SENTENCE DICTATION

1. ______________________________
2. ______________________________
3. ______________________________
4. ______________________________
5. ______________________________
6. ______________________________
7. ______________________________
8. ______________________________
9. ______________________________
10. ______________________________

E. PROBLEM WORDS

1. ______________
2. ______________
3. ______________
4. ______________
5. ______________

F.

FILL IN THE BLANKS WITH YOUR SPELLING WORDS

If you ______ yourself it is very important to do some things. First you have to ______ an open cut. The sore place can become infected if ______ gets into it. ______ cuts can cause trouble. If you think you broke a bone, do ______ until a doctor sees it. ______ you are waiting for help, try to stay as still as possible.

G.

MAKING SENTENCES

1. clean / dirty / your

1. ____________________

2. nothing / do / while

2. ____________________

H.

MY OWN WRITING

Tell about a time you got hurt badly.

____

I.

WHICH ONE SHOULD YOU USE?

by buy

1. Which one shall we ______?
2. Shall we go ______ plane or ______ train?
3. Did your mother ______ you that new radio?
4. Let's pass ______ the mall on the way home.
5. If we go to the market ______ car we can ______ more things.

HOW YOU DID

Spelling ______

	Super	Good	Getting Better	Needs Lots of Work
Punctuation				
Appearance				
Creativity				

LESSON 14

A. SPELL YOUR NEW WORDS

1. ______
2. ______
3. ______
4. ______
5. ______
6. ______
7. ______
8. ______

B. FILL IN THE BLANKS WITH YOUR SPELLING WORDS

1. The cake tastes ______ than the pie.
2. I've never heard anyone ______ for ______ a long time.
3. You may ______ the puppy if you will take care of him.
4. Sue ______ for ten minutes until she ______ her lost ring.
5. Can you hear the kitten ______ in her box?

C. PUT YOUR SPELLING WORDS IN ABC ORDER

1. ______
2. ______
3. ______
4. ______
5. ______
6. ______
7. ______
8. ______

D. SENTENCE DICTATION

1. ______
2. ______
3. ______
4. ______
5. ______
6. ______
7. ______
8. ______
9. ______
10. ______

E. PROBLEM WORDS

1. ______
2. ______
3. ______
4. ______
5. ______

F.

FILL IN THE BLANKS WITH YOUR SPELLING WORDS

One day while I was walking I ________ a small gold locket on the ground. It was ____________ a pretty locket that I wanted to ________ it. But when I got to the corner I saw a little girl __________ . She cried and ________. I asked what was wrong. She said she had lost her locket and it was a special present from her grandmother. "Don't ______," I said. "I think you will feel much __________ when you see what's in my hand." The smile on her face made me feel really good, even if I didn't get to keep the locket.

G.

MAKING SENTENCES

1. keep / found / great

1. ____

____

2. cried / because / such

2. ____

____

H.

MY OWN WRITING

____

Choose a person you know and describe what he or she looks like and what that person is like.

____

____

____

____

____

I.

WHICH ONE SHOULD YOU USE?

where were

1. What ________ you doing over there?

2. We didn't see ________ you ________ going.

3. Do you know ________ she put my radio?

4. They ________ all going for a bike ride.

5. ________ do you think they ________ having lunch?

HOW YOU DID

Spelling ____________

	Super	Good	Getting Better	Needs Lots of Work
Punctuation				
Appearance				
Creativity				

LESSON 15

A. SPELL YOUR NEW WORDS

1. ______
2. ______
3. ______
4. ______
5. ______
6. ______

B. FILL IN THE BLANKS WITH YOUR SPELLING WORDS

1. I think yellow would be a nice ______ to paint your room.
2. I hope you will be ______ to your cousin.
3. There are 52 weeks in a ______ .
4. We ______ in each ______ of the year with different crayons.
5. I hope you won't have ______ with that new boy.

C. WHAT CONTRACTION COULD YOU USE INSTEAD

She would love to go.

We would be early if we left now.

I would like to play too.

You would be angry if I said that.

They would come if they could.

D. SENTENCE DICTATION

1. ______
2. ______
3. ______
4. ______
5. ______
6. ______
7. ______
8. ______
9. ______
10. ______

E. PROBLEM WORDS

1. ______
2. ______
3. ______
4. ______
5. ______

F.

FILL IN THE BLANKS WITH YOUR SPELLING WORDS

Sometimes I have __________ getting things done. This year I decided to really get myself together and plan my life. First I made this ________ big calendar with 12 pages, one for each _________ . Then I drew in the weeks and __________ in the weekends and holidays in yellow. Each week I listed which days I would do my chores and what days I would go to my scout meetings or do my lawn jobs. I did each of these in a different ________. Then I could tell which days would be better for my big homework projects. I think it will be a better ________ this way.

G.

MAKING SENTENCES

1. each / month / better

1. ______________________________

2. draw / color / paper

2. ______________________________

H.

MY OWN WRITING

Tell about what you did during your last vacation.

I.

WHICH ONE SHOULD YOU USE?

no know now

1. I don't ________ which to do first.
2. My father said ________ when I asked for a new radio.
3. Do you ________ Mr. Green?
4. Can we go ________?
5. ________ you may not go ________.

HOW YOU DID

Spelling ________

Super	Good	Getting Better	Needs Lots of Work

Punctuation

Appearance

Creativity

LESSON 16

A. SPELL YOUR NEW WORDS

1. ______
2. ______
3. ______
4. ______
5. ______
6. ______

B. FILL IN THE BLANKS WITH YOUR SPELLING WORDS

1. I think you're the best mom in the ______ .
2. The boy bumped his ______ on a branch.
3. I would love to eat a ______ of those grapes but I ______ have any room left.
4. We thought you already ______ the answer.
5. I wonder if there is ______ on any other planet.

C. WHICH IS RIGHT?

go goes
going went

Did she ______ with him?

How are they ______ home?

We all ______ home together yesterday.

She ______ to the mall every day.

D. SENTENCE DICTATION

1. ______
2. ______
3. ______
4. ______
5. ______
6. ______
7. ______
8. ______
9. ______
10. ______

E. PROBLEM WORDS

1. ______
2. ______
3. ______
4. ______
5. ______

F.

FILL IN THE BLANKS WITH YOUR SPELLING WORDS

If you _______ what my _______ was like you would feel sorry for me. It's so crowded in my house that we keep bumping into each other. A _______ of my brothers and sisters have rooms of their own, but most of us share. I sleep on the bottom of a bunk bed and always bump my _______ when I get up. I can _______ ever find a quiet corner to do my homework. I must find a place in this _______ where I can be alone sometimes.

G.

MAKING SENTENCES

1. knew / world / about

1. ______________________________

2. few / people / life

2. ______________________________

H.

MY OWN WRITING

Tell what you would like to do for your next vacation.

I.

WHICH ONE SHOULD YOU USE?

1. Do you know how this _______ ? (work / works)
2. All these people _______ chocolate ice cream. (like / likes)
3. I don't think he _______ her. (know / knows)
4. The boys _______ prizes when they win a race. (get / gets)
5. She really _______ hard but she isn't learning it. (try / tries)

HOW YOU DID

Spelling _______

	Super	Good	Getting Better	Needs Lots of Work
Punctuation				
Appearance				
Creativity				

LESSON 17

A. SPELL YOUR NEW WORDS

1. ______________
2. ______________
3. ______________
4. ______________
5. ______________
6. ______________

B. FILL IN THE BLANKS WITH YOUR SPELLING WORDS

1. Are you all ________ to go to the beach yet?
2. I'm not ________ to dive into the pool any more.
3. The plant will ________ better in the sunlight.
4. Thank goodness my homework is done ________ .
5. We ________ wait ________ your brother gets home.

C. WHICH IS RIGHT?

give gives
giving gave

He______ his old bike to his brother.

Are you ______ us a test today?

I won't ______ away my old dolls.

My mom ______ me lunch every day.

D. SENTENCE DICTATION

1. ______________________________
2. ______________________________
3. ______________________________
4. ______________________________
5. ______________________________
6. ______________________________
7. ______________________________
8. ______________________________
9. ______________________________
10. ______________________________

E. PROBLEM WORDS

1. ______________
2. ______________
3. ______________
4. ______________
5. ______________

F.

FILL IN THE BLANKS WITH YOUR SPELLING WORDS

I hate being so tall. I'm only ten years old and I'm ________ 5 feet 7 inches. That's a lot for a girl. I'm taller than most of the boys. Some kids tease me. They call me "bean pole" or "string bean." And the doctor says I'm not ________ to stop growing yet. He thinks I ________ probably ________ another two or three inches and I'm ________ he's right. My mother says it may seem bad now but it will be great when I'm a woman. I sure hope she's right. But it will be hard to wait ________ then.

G.

MAKING SENTENCES

1. afraid / ready / school

1. ____

2. until / shall / grow

2. ____

H.

MY OWN WRITING

Tell about something real you are afraid of. Tell why you are afraid and how it makes you feel.

____

____

I.

WHICH ONE SHOULD YOU USE?

right write

1. Come here ________ now.
2. Turn ________ at the next corner.
3. Let's ________ this down before we forget it.
4. I don't know which is the ________ one.
5. I have to ________ a letter to my aunt.

HOW YOU DID

Spelling ________

	Super	Good	Getting Better	Needs Lots of Work
Punctuation				
Appearance				
Creativity				

LESSON 18

A. SPELL YOUR NEW WORDS

1. ________
2. ________
3. ________
4. ________
5. ________
6. ________
7. ________

B. FILL IN THE BLANKS WITH YOUR SPELLING WORDS

1. Please ______ the oven and put in the pie.
2. The pet store was ________ by the time we got there.
3. Here's a good ______ for our _________ to have a picnic.
4. If you come too _______ to me I might catch your cold.
5. They have ________ a new restaurant ________ the corner.

C. WHICH IS RIGHT?

have has having had

We are________ breakfast late today.

We ________ not been home yet today.

I ________ a bad day yesterday.

She ________ a new friend.

D. SENTENCE DICTATION

____

1. ________

____

2. ________

____

3. ________

____

4. ________

____

5. ________

____

6. ________

____

7. ________

____

8. ________

____

9. ________

____

10. ________

____

E. PROBLEM WORDS

1. ________
2. ________
3. ________
4. ________
5. ________

F. FILL IN THE BLANKS WITH YOUR SPELLING WORDS

I already told you that I wish I had a ________ of my own to go to sometimes. There's no place ________ here where I can be alone. My mother doesn't like us to lock doors. So if I ________ a door to keep people out, someone in the ________ will ________ it. Last night I went into the bathroom to try to read. First my little brother ________ the door and just walked in. So I pushed him out and ________ the door again. After the third time this happened I hung up a sign saying "Closed For Repairs."

G. MAKING SENTENCES

1. place / around / here

1. ____

____

2. opened / close / please

2. ____

____

H. MY OWN WRITING

____

Describe your family.

____

____

____

____

I.

WHICH ONE SHOULD YOU USE?

was were

1. My sister and I ________ working in the kitchen.
2. She ________ showing me how to bake a cake.
3. We ________ almost done when my mother came home.
4. "What ________ you two doing?" she asked.
5. Mom ________ happy when she saw what we ________ doing.

HOW YOU DID

Spelling ________

	Super	Good	Getting Better	Needs Lots of Work
Punctuation				
Appearance				
Creativity				

LESSON 19

A. SPELL YOUR NEW WORDS

1. ______
2. ______
3. ______
4. ______
5. ______
6. ______
7. ______
8. ______

B. FILL IN THE BLANKS WITH YOUR SPELLING WORDS

1. The brown cow is ______ into the barn.
2. This ______ of my hair goes to the ______ side.
3. They had to ______ a long way to get to the ______.
4. A very ______ girl ______ onto the stage.
5. I can't hear a ______ that you're saying.

C. PUT YOUR SPELLING WORDS IN ABC ORDER

1. ______
2. ______
3. ______
4. ______
5. ______
6. ______
7. ______
8. ______

D. SENTENCE DICTATION

1. ______
2. ______
3. ______
4. ______
5. ______
6. ______
7. ______
8. ______
9. ______
10. ______

E. PROBLEM WORDS

1. ______
2. ______
3. ______
4. ______
5. ______

F.

FILL IN THE BLANKS WITH YOUR SPELLING WORDS

I like to ________ into town. Last week I was __________ around the mall when I saw this really pretty girl. I __________ up to her and asked if she would like to have a soda with me. She said, "Sure!" But that was the last ________ she said until we ________ the soda shop. And besides, she only had ________ of her soda. Maybe she was just shy. But even if she was ________, she wasn't much fun. So I don't think I'll ask her to my ________ next week.

G.

MAKING SENTENCES

1. pretty
   soon
   walk

1. ______________________________

2. left
   part
   homework

2. ______________________________

H.

MY OWN WRITING

Write about a favorite place of yours. Describe it.

I.

WHICH ONE SHOULD YOU USE?

there their they're

(place)
1. Can we go ________ after dinner?

(they are)
2. ________ very nice people.

(belongs to them)
3. They want us to come to ________ home tonight.

(they are)
4. I think ________ going to be home tonight.

(place)
5. What have you got in ________.

HOW YOU DID

Spelling ________

	Super	Good	Getting Better	Needs Lots of Work
Punctuation				
Appearance				
Creativity				

LESSON 20

A. SPELL YOUR NEW WORDS

1. ____________
2. ____________
3. ____________
4. ____________
5. ____________
6. ____________
7. ____________

B. FILL IN THE BLANKS WITH YOUR SPELLING WORDS

1. If you ________ to me I can't hear the teacher.
2. Driving a ________ car saves money on gas.
3. I'm so hot. Did you ________ anything ________ to drink?
4. We all ________ about how ________ the summer was.
5. Just ________ about winter days makes me feel cold.

C. WHICH IS RIGHT?

do does doing did

She always ________ all the work the teacher gives us.

I was ________ my best.

He never ________ anything wrong before.

What did you ______ with that ball?

E. PROBLEM WORDS

1. ____________
2. ____________
3. ____________
4. ____________
5. ____________

D. SENTENCE DICTATION

1. ____________
2. ____________
3. ____________
4. ____________
5. ____________
6. ____________
7. ____________
8. ____________
9. ____________
10. ____________

F.

FILL IN THE BLANKS WITH YOUR SPELLING WORDS

One day we were ________ about the kinds of houses people live in. Our teacher ________ about how ________ most houses are in other parts of the world. Many houses have only one room. In ________ countries some houses are made of grass and some of mud. This helps the people keep cool. Where it's very ________ people sit around a fire in the middle of the room. They ________ their food around the fire where the whole family sits to eat and ________.

G.

MAKING SENTENCES

1. bring, talking, about

1. ____________________
____
____

2. some, cold, small

2. ____________________
____

H.

MY OWN WRITING

Tell about something your parents want you to do, or that they expect that you don't want to do.

____
____
____
____
____

I.

WHICH ONE SHOULD YOU USE?

would wood

1. What ________ you like to do tonight?
2. I ________ like to make a boat out of ________.
3. Some ________ on our house is starting to rot.
4. Which one ________ you like to have?
5. ________ you please take this piece of ________ outside.

HOW YOU DID

Spelling ________

	Super	Good	Getting Better	Needs Lots of Work
Punctuation				
Appearance				
Creativity				

LESSON 21

A. SPELL YOUR NEW WORDS

1. ____________
2. ____________
3. ____________
4. ____________
5. ____________
6. ____________
7. ____________

B. FILL IN THE BLANKS WITH YOUR SPELLING WORDS

1. Last week we ________ at a circus clown.
2. If today is Monday then __________ was Sunday.
3. I _______ think your jokes are ________.
4. Please don't ________ at me when I sing __________.
5. Were you __________ at me when I slipped on the ice?

C. WHAT CONTRACTION COULD YOU USE INSTEAD

She had been to California before.

They had taken the best seats.

We had better be going.

You had eaten it all before I even started.

I had finished it already.

D. SENTENCE DICTATION

1. ____________________
2. ____________________
3. ____________________
4. ____________________
5. ____________________
6. ____________________
7. ____________________
8. ____________________
9. ____________________
10. ____________________

E. PROBLEM WORDS

1. ____________
2. ____________
3. ____________
4. ____________
5. ____________

F.

FILL IN THE BLANKS WITH YOUR SPELLING WORDS

This week we are taking turns giving talks in front of the class. __________ it was my friend, Tom's turn. Well, he didn't mean to be funny but he did say some pretty ________ things and the kids were real mean and they __________ at him. I can ________ see his face and how unhappy he was when they were __________ . It will be my turn ____________ and I just hope no one will ________ at me.

G.

MAKING SENTENCES

1. still / laughing / funny

2. yesterday / but / tomorrow

1. ____

____

2. ____

____

H.

MY OWN WRITING

If you could do anything you liked tomorrow what would you do? Describe your day.

I.

WHICH ONE SHOULD YOU USE?

is are was were

1. ________ you reading that book yesterday?
2. Where ________ you going now?
3. How many marbles ________ in the box when you opened it?
4. She ________ the first to finish the dishes last night.
5. There ________ too much work to do right now.

HOW YOU DID

Spelling __________

	Super	Good	Getting Better	Needs Lots of Work
Punctuation				
Appearance				
Creativity				

LESSON 22

A. SPELL YOUR NEW WORDS

1. ______________
2. ______________
3. ______________
4. ______________
5. ______________
6. ______________
7. ______________

C. WHICH IS RIGHT?

feel feels feeling felt

How do you ________ today?

I am ________ great right now.

But I ________ terrible yesterday.

At this moment she ________ fine.

E. PROBLEM WORDS

1. ______________
2. ______________
3. ______________
4. ______________
5. ______________

B. FILL IN THE BLANKS WITH YOUR SPELLING WORDS

1. Be very ________ when you learn to drive.
2. Do you ________ that I can pass this test?
3. You must ______ smoking if you ______ about your health.
4. I failed the test because I was ________ .
5. Please ________ out or ________ you might fall.

D. SENTENCE DICTATION

1. ______________
2. ______________
3. ______________
4. ______________
5. ______________
6. ______________
7. ______________
8. ______________
9. ______________
10. ______________

F. FILL IN THE BLANKS WITH YOUR SPELLING WORDS

I've been having some trouble in school. I'm getting behind in my work. My teacher says my writing is getting __________ and I had better __________ out. My father thinks I'm fooling around and he says I had better ________ wasting time or ________ I'll be in big trouble. I do ________ about my work and I am trying to be __________ . But there are some things that are hard for me and writing is one of them. I sure wish he would __________ me.

G. MAKING SENTENCES

1. watch / don't / careless

1. ______________________________

____

2. better / believe / else

2. ______________________________

____

H. MY OWN WRITING

Write about something people believe that you don't (like witches or flying saucers.)

____

____

____

____

____

I. WHICH ONE SHOULD YOU USE?

then than

1. I like chocolate better ________ vanilla.
2. Soon it will be late. ________ we won't be able to go out.
3. If you go, ________ I can go too.
4. Is his car in worse shape ________ ours?
5. If your bike is worse ________ mine, ________ you had better get a new one.

HOW YOU DID

Spelling ____________

	Super	Good	Getting Better	Needs Lots of Work
Punctuation				
Appearance				
Creativity				

LESSON 23

A. SPELL YOUR NEW WORDS

1. ____________
2. ____________
3. ____________
4. ____________
5. ____________
6. ____________
7. ____________

B. FILL IN THE BLANKS WITH YOUR SPELLING WORDS

1. I often ________ how many stars there are.
2. The show will ________ when everyone is quiet.
3. The ________world is ________ a little every day.
4. May we go to the beach ________ of the park?
5. We're going to have to ________ some of these wrong answers.

C. WHICH IS RIGHT?

take takes
taking took

Last night she ________ home all her books.

We are ________ him to school now.

Don't ________ that cookie.

That dog ________ his bone wherever he goes.

D. SENTENCE DICTATION

1. ____________
2. ____________
3. ____________
4. ____________
5. ____________
6. ____________
7. ____________
8. ____________
9. ____________
10. ____________

E. PROBLEM WORDS

1. ____________
2. ____________
3. ____________
4. ____________
5. ____________

F.

FILL IN THE BLANKS WITH YOUR SPELLING WORDS

My mother decided that __________ of buying vegetables this year we should grow our own. She wants to ________ almost our ________ garden into a small farm. First we had to get the ground ready. Now we are planting the seeds. I really like this kind of work but I __________ how long it will be before things will ________ to grow. Maybe the seeds are __________ into little seedlings already.

G.

MAKING SENTENCES

1. change instead one

1. ______________________________

2. wonder start when

2. ______________________________

H.

MY OWN WRITING

Tell some things you could do for fun besides watching TV.

I.

WHICH ONE SHOULD YOU USE?

went gone

1. Has Timmy ________ to school yet?
2. They ________ with me to the park.
3. I have ________ to the market twice today.
4. We had only ________ a little way when we met her.
5. They all ________ home early yesterday.

HOW YOU DID

Spelling ________

	Super	Good	Getting Better	Needs Lots of Work
Punctuation				
Appearance				
Creativity				

LESSON 24

A. SPELL YOUR NEW WORDS

1. ____________________
2. ____________________
3. ____________________
4. ____________________
5. ____________________
6. ____________________
7. ____________________
8. ____________________

B. FILL IN THE BLANKS WITH YOUR SPELLING WORDS

1. Is that fruit ________ or made of plastic?
2. I want to ________ you for a ________ nice day.
3. We should ________ the food ________ before it rains.
4. The pine tree ________ our house is quite old.
5. The right ________ of our car has a dent in it.

C. WHICH IS RIGHT?

tell tells telling told

________ me another story.

I ________ her not to call me any more.

They were ________ a ghost story.

She ________ me that all the time.

D. SENTENCE DICTATION

1. ____
2. ____
3. ____
4. ____
5. ____
6. ____
7. ____
8. ____
9. ____
10. ____

E. PROBLEM WORDS

1. ____________________
2. ____________________
3. ____________________
4. ____________________
5. ____________________

F.

FILL IN THE BLANKS WITH YOUR SPELLING WORDS

I know it sounds funny, but my family is moving to the other ________ of our street. We have to ________ because we have a new baby and this house is just too small. But we ________ like our neighbors and don't want to leave this neighborhood. So we found a house on the same block. The ________ looks about the same with white paint and a porch and big trees. But the ________ is much bigger with a ________ fireplace. And ________ goodness, I'll have a room of my own.

G.

MAKING SENTENCES

1. move / inside / if

1. ____

2. really / thank / for

2. ____

H.

MY OWN WRITING

Describe your favorite month of the year.

____

I.

WHICH ONE SHOULD YOU USE?

your   you're   yours

1. Is that ________ paper on my desk?
2. No, it's ________ .
3. ________ the one who put it there.
4. I don't think ________ very nice to me.
5. Which new book of ________ is the one ________ going to read next?

HOW YOU DID

Spelling ________

	Super	Good	Getting Better	Needs Lots of Work
Punctuation				
Appearance				
Creativity				

LESSON 25

A. SPELL YOUR NEW WORDS

1. ______
2. ______
3. ______
4. ______
5. ______
6. ______

B. FILL IN THE BLANKS WITH YOUR SPELLING WORDS

1. Did you ______ to ______ what the president said?
2. If you eat candy and cake too ______ you'll get fat.
3. What ______ at the end of the story?
4. I just ______ that it might snow tomorrow.
5. Sometimes when I wake up it isn't even ______ yet.

C. PUT YOUR SPELLING WORDS IN ABC ORDER

1. ______
2. ______
3. ______
4. ______
5. ______
6. ______

D. SENTENCE DICTATION

1. ______
2. ______
3. ______
4. ______
5. ______
6. ______
7. ______
8. ______
9. ______
10. ______

E. PROBLEM WORDS

1. ______
2. ______
3. ______
4. ______
5. ______

F.

FILL IN THE BLANKS WITH YOUR SPELLING WORDS

Did you ______ about Maria? I don't know what will ________ to her. Her mother always tells her to come home when it's still ________ out. Well, she doesn't always listen to her mother and she ________ gets home after dark these days. And yesterday I ________ that she has been getting into trouble. I know she got home late and her mother was very angry. I don't think anything __________ this time, but if she isn't careful I hear that her mother won't let her go out any more.

G.

MAKING SENTENCES

1. heard / happened / something

1. ______________________________

2. often / hear / don't

2. ______________________________

H.

MY OWN WRITING

People worry about different things at different times in their lives, write about something that worries you.

____

I.

WHICH ONE SHOULD YOU USE?

here hear

1. Did you ______ that rock concert last night?
2. The rock group is coming ______ next year.
3. ______ we are at the beach and it's raining.
4. We couldn't ______ what you were saying.
5. Didn't you ______ me ask you to come over ______?

HOW YOU DID

Spelling ______

	Super	Good	Getting Better	Needs Lots of Work
Punctuation				
Appearance				
Creativity				

LESSON 26

A. SPELL YOUR NEW WORDS

1. ______
2. ______
3. ______
4. ______
5. ______
6. ______
7. ______

B FILL IN THE BLANKS WITH YOUR SPELLING WORDS

1. How ______ do we have to wait until lunch?
2. My little brother likes me to ______ him on the swing.
3. Let's ______ the wagon ______ the sidewalk.
4. May I help you ______ those bags?
5. ______ of us have visited any other ______ .

C. WHAT CONTRACTION COULD YOU USE INSTEAD?

Sue **has not** been to see her grandmother all week.

Her grandmother **was not** home when she got there.

She **does not** want to go.

He **is not** going to stay home just to see Jose.

They **are not** coming today.

D. SENTENCE DICTATION

1. ______
2. ______
3. ______
4. ______
5. ______
6. ______
7. ______
8. ______
9. ______
10. ______

E. PROBLEM WORDS

1. ______
2. ______
3. ______
4. ______
5. ______

F.

FILL IN THE BLANKS WITH YOUR SPELLING WORDS

It's a _______ way from my house to the market and part of it is uphill. My mom often sends me to get something she needs because she works and doesn't have much time. And if _______ of my sisters are home, sometimes she makes me take my little brother _______ to give her time to make dinner. What a pest! First I _______ him up the hill in his wagon. Then I have to _______ him back down. And I even have to _______ the food because he knocks everything out of the wagon. I think I'll learn to carry things on my head like they do in other _______ .

G.

MAKING SENTENCES

1. pull / along / with

1. ______________________________

____

2. carry / much / far

2. ______________________________

____

H.

MY OWN WRITING

____

Tell about a time you got caught telling a lie. Tell what happened and how it made you feel.

____

____

____

____

I.

WHICH ONE SHOULD YOU USE?

do did done

1. We have _______ all our work for today.
2. She _______ her school work very well.
3. Did you _______ everything you were supposed to?
4. I don't know what he _______ to his bike.
5. What has she _______ with my new dress?

HOW YOU DID

Spelling _______

Super	Good	Getting Better	Needs Lots of Work

Punctuation

Appearance

Creativity

LESSON 27

A. SPELL YOUR NEW WORDS

1. ______
2. ______
3. ______
4. ______
5. ______
6. ______

B. FILL IN THE BLANKS WITH YOUR SPELLING WORDS

1. I ______ you were going to ______ for me.
2. Would you like a little ______ of this cake?
3. I hate it when they leave me home ______.
4. The train moved ______ along the track.
5. Please ______ down a little. You talk too fast.

C. WHICH IS RIGHT?

think thinks
thinking thought

Penny ______ she can sing better than I can.
Mark ______ he could beat me but he couldn't.
Are you ______ what I am?
They______they are smarter but they aren't.

D. SENTENCE DICTATION

1. ______
2. ______
3. ______
4. ______
5. ______
6. ______
7. ______
8. ______
9. ______
10. ______

E. PROBLEM WORDS

1. ______
2. ______
3. ______
4. ______
5. ______

F.

FILL IN THE BLANKS WITH YOUR SPELLING WORDS

I love chocolate but I always have some problems when I buy a chocolate bar. First, I like to be ________ when I eat it because I don't want to share and I know that isn't nice. Then I like to ________ a while between bites so I don't eat it all at once. I try to be so ________, and eat one little ________ at a time so it will last forever. But, of course, it doesn't. And every time I say the same thing to myself. "I never ________ I could eat so ________ and that chocolate could still go so fast."

G.

MAKING SENTENCES

1. wait, very, slowly

1. ____

2. yesterday, thought, piece

2. ____

H.

MY OWN WRITING

Tell about how you feel when you are home alone at night, or when you are alone in the dark.

____

____

____

____

I.

WHICH ONE SHOULD YOU USE?

isn't aren't

1. ________ they coming tonight?

2. No, they ________ coming until tomorrow.

3. ________ Nancy working with us?

4. Paul ________ doing that right.

5. Why ________ James and Andy here yet?

HOW YOU DID

Spelling ________

	Super	Good	Getting Better	Needs Lots of Work
Punctuation				
Appearance				
Creativity				

LESSON 28

A. SPELL YOUR NEW WORDS

1. ____________
2. ____________
3. ____________
4. ____________
5. ____________
6. ____________
7. ____________

B. FILL IN THE BLANKS WITH YOUR SPELLING WORDS

1. You can ________ here until dinner time.
2. That jet looks so ______ in the sky.
3. The ________ is so cold today ________ freeze if we go in.
4. Turn the radio down ________, please.
5. Someday ________ learn to ______ a plane.

C. WHICH CONTRACTION SHOULD YOU USE

If **you will** go with me I'll buy you a soda.

I will be upset if she doesn't take me along.

We will go now if you will.

Father said **they will** go.

I don't think **he will** do that any more.

D. SENTENCE DICTATION

1. ____________
2. ____________
3. ____________
4. ____________
5. ____________
6. ____________
7. ____________
8. ____________
9. ____________
10. ____________

E. PROBLEM WORDS

1. ____________
2. ____________
3. ____________
4. ____________
5. ____________

F.

FILL IN THE BLANKS WITH YOUR SPELLING WORDS

Did you ever see a seaplane? It can take off and land in the ________. Instead of wheels it has something called pontoons that are flat and can help the plane ________ on top of the water. Most seaplanes are small. They can ________ pretty ________ up, but often they fly ________ over the water. They need seaplanes in places where there is no flat land for a landing strip. Maybe one day ________ get to fly in one.

G.

MAKING SENTENCES

1. stay / water / please

1. ____

____

____

2. fly / high / great

2. ____

____

H.

MY OWN WRITING

Imagine that you can fly. Tell what it is like.

____

____

____

____

____

I.

WHICH ONE SHOULD YOU USE?

hasn't haven't

1. ________ Mrs. Green put today's lesson on the board yet?
2. Our state ________ got such bad weather.
3. Those people ________ the time to help us.
4. That house ________ as many trees as ours.
5. We ________ any place to go today.

HOW YOU DID

Spelling ________

Super	Good	Getting Better	Needs Lots of Work

Punctuation

Appearance

Creativity

LESSON 29

A. SPELL YOUR NEW WORDS

1. ________
2. ________
3. ________
4. ________
5. ________
6. ________

B. FILL IN THE BLANKS WITH YOUR SPELLING WORDS

1. I'm too ________ to talk to you now.
2. I can't ________ if I want the red one or the blue one.
3. Are you ________ that Mr. Parks is your new teacher?
4. I would like to go into town even ________ it's late.
5. Be sure to cross the ________ at the corner.

C. WHICH IS RIGHT?

cry cries
crying cried

The movie was so sad I felt like ________.

I'll really be upset if she ________.

I ________ a long time when my uncle died.

Please don't ________ any more.

D. SENTENCE DICTATION

1. ________
2. ________
3. ________
4. ________
5. ________
6. ________
7. ________
8. ________
9. ________
10. ________

E. PROBLEM WORDS

1. ________
2. ________
3. ________
4. ________
5. ________

F.

FILL IN THE BLANKS WITH YOUR SPELLING WORDS

Big city streets are so ________ . If you come from a small town to visit the city, it's a little scary. I'm never ________ which way to go to get around. And there are never so many people on the ________ at home. But even ________ it's crowded my family loves the city. There's so much to see and do that we never can ________ what to do first. This morning we are going to visit a museum. Then we'll go to the zoo. And later this evening we're going to see the biggest circus in the world.

G.

MAKING SENTENCES

1. wait / later / decide

1. ____

2. busy / though / street

2. ____

H.

MY OWN WRITING

Your mother says you can decide whether you want to do your chores now or later. How do you decide?

____

I.

WHICH ONE SHOULD YOU USE?

doesn't   don't

1. ________ you like her any more?
2. His friend ________ like me very much.
3. ________ her mother work at night?
4. She ________ take her piano lesson until tomorrow.
5. We ________ think you should go today.

HOW YOU DID

Spelling ________

	Super	Good	Getting Better	Needs Lots of Work
Punctuation				
Appearance				
Creativity				

LESSON 30

A. SPELL YOUR NEW WORDS

1. ______
2. ______
3. ______
4. ______
5. ______
6. ______

B. FILL IN THE BLANKS WITH YOUR SPELLING WORDS

1. When you are ______ working you may go out.
2. My dog sleeps ______ my bed.
3. I really didn't ______ to hurt her.
4. Winning that race ______ a lot to me.
5. I ______ we can ______ this game later.

C. WHICH IS RIGHT?

buy buys
buying bought

What are you ______ now?

Did she ______ one or two?

My family ______ a new house.

He ______ a piece of candy every day.

D. SENTENCE DICTATION

1. ______
2. ______
3. ______
4. ______
5. ______
6. ______
7. ______
8. ______
9. ______
10. ______

E. PROBLEM WORDS

1. ______
2. ______
3. ______
4. ______
5. ______

F.

FILL IN THE BLANKS WITH YOUR SPELLING WORDS

I always_________to get my work done before I go out to play. But sometimes I just don't feel like doing it, so I leave some to _________ later. Well, yesterday I _________ to finish a book report but my friend Kim came over and said, "Let's go out." I put the report _________ some papers on my desk so my mother couldn't see that it wasn't _________. Then when I came home I forgot all about it. The next day I was in trouble in school. So I _________ I will stick to my motto, "Work first. Play later."

G.

MAKING SENTENCES

1. now, guess, finished

1. ____________________

2. didn't, mean, under

2. ____________________

H.

MY OWN WRITING

Write about what you think you would like to be some day. Include why you chose that.

I.

WHICH ONE SHOULD YOU USE?

anything nothing

1. Can't you do _________ right?
2. There's _________ I can do about that.
3. I can't get _________ on here to work.
4. Don't do _________ you'll be sorry for.
5. There's _________ left to eat in the refrigerator.

HOW YOU DID

Spelling _________

	Super	Good	Getting Better	Needs Lots of Work
Punctuation				
Appearance				
Creativity				

LESSON 31

A. SPELL YOUR NEW WORDS

1. ____________
2. ____________
3. ____________
4. ____________
5. ____________
6. ____________

B. FILL IN THE BLANKS WITH YOUR SPELLING WORDS

1. In the ____________ I can hear so many birds singing.
2. They went to the store and ____________ some socks.
3. Everyone knew the ____________ to his question.
4. Her new coat is ____________ than her old one.
5. My grandfather ________ some great cookies with him when he came to our house.

C. WHICH IS RIGHT?

bring brings
bringing brought

We all ____________ snacks for the party last night.

They were ____________ their friends a gift.

Did you ________ back my book?

She ____________ me flowers every morning.

D. SENTENCE DICTATION

1. ____________
2. ____________
3. ____________
4. ____________
5. ____________
6. ____________
7. ____________
8. ____________
9. ____________
10. ____________

E. PROBLEM WORDS

1. ____________
2. ____________
3. ____________
4. ____________
5. ____________

F. FILL IN THE BLANKS WITH YOUR SPELLING WORDS

What a beautiful __________ this is. It is __________ than last week and I love these summer days. When it's very __________ I feel as if I could just swim all day. When I swim I like to look at the fish and see if I can find their names in my fish book. My sister __________ me new fins and a swim mask and I __________ them down to the beach yesterday. It was great. I saw this fantastic new fish, but I don't know what it is. Maybe my book will have the __________.

G. MAKING SENTENCES

1. please / answer / asked

1. ______________________________

2. morning / brought / with

2. ______________________________

H. MY OWN WRITING

Tell about the best thing anyone ever bought you.

I. REWRITE THE SENTENCES

(sentences can vary)

1. I very unhappy.
2. You want go market.
3. You me can tennis play.
4. We been gone to the movies.
5. Them people very fast walk.

HOW YOU DID

Spelling __________

	Super	Good	Getting Better	Needs Lots of Work
Punctuation				
Appearance				
Creativity				

LESSON 32

A. SPELL YOUR NEW WORDS

1. ____________
2. ____________
3. ____________
4. ____________
5. ____________
6. ____________
7. ____________
8. ____________

B. FILL IN THE BLANKS WITH YOUR SPELLING WORDS

1. Are you________kind to those children?
2. I________you will________with my plan.
3. I don't like it when we__________about so many things.
4. We had ________she would come sometime ________the day, but she didn't.
5. He leaned the ladder__________the tree.

C. WHICH IS RIGHT?

write writes
writing wrote

I'm not __________ to her any more.

Last week we __________ to our pen pals.

You __________ too slowly.

My brother __________ to me every day.

D. SENTENCE DICTATION

1. ____________
2. ____________
3. ____________
4. ____________
5. ____________
6. ____________
7. ____________
8. ____________
9. ____________
10. ____________

E. PROBLEM WORDS

1. ____________
2. ____________
3. ____________
4. ____________
5. ____________

F. FILL IN THE BLANKS WITH YOUR SPELLING WORDS

There are so many things people don't ________ about and then they fight. If I'm for something, and you're ________ it, why can't we just talk about it? Usually ________ an argument people get angry with each other instead of ________ friendly and trying to listen to what the other person is saying. I ________ that if you ________ with me, you will at least listen to my side of the story.

G. MAKING SENTENCES

1. disagree / about / why

1. ____

2. during / were / being

2. ____

H. MY OWN WRITING

Tell about something you would like me (the teacher) to do differently.

I. REWRITE THE SENTENCES

(sentences can vary)

1. Me like play ball.
2. That car too fast go.
3. You work market?
4. That job no good.
5. Where gone children?

HOW YOU DID

Spelling ________

	Super	Good	Getting Better	Needs Lots of Work
Punctuation				
Appearance				
Creativity				

LESSON 33

A. SPELL YOUR NEW WORDS

1. ______
2. ______
3. ______
4. ______
5. ______
6. ______
7. ______

B. FILL IN THE BLANKS WITH YOUR SPELLING WORDS

1. The sun is much larger than the ______.
2. There should be no ______ during a fire drill.
3. There will be a race ______ the first and the ______ graders.
4. Hold your paper correctly before you ______ to write.
5. In the ______ of the year our class was too ______.

C. WHICH IS RIGHT?

sleep sleeps
sleeping slept

______ so late isn't good for you.

We all ______ at our aunt's house last night.

Do you always dream when you ______?

He ______ at our house when he's in town.

D. SENTENCE DICTATION

1. ______
2. ______
3. ______
4. ______
5. ______
6. ______
7. ______
8. ______
9. ______
10. ______

E. PROBLEM WORDS

1. ______
2. ______
3. ______
4. ______
5. ______

F. FILL IN THE BLANKS WITH YOUR SPELLING WORDS

Sometimes it's so ________ around here that I can't stand it. In school, __________ the kids talking and fighting and teachers trying to quiet them down, I can't pay attention. It's not just in school. Some people play their radios and TV so loud it blasts my ears. I keep hearing fighting and yelling all over. It's __________ to really upset me. To ________ with, the ________ would be a much better place if people would think about how bad the ________ is for themselves. And ________, if they would think about how it bothers others.

G. MAKING SENTENCES

1. begin / first / second

1. ____________________

2. fly / between / earth

2. ____________________

H. MY OWN WRITING

Tell how you think the earth is changing because of what people are doing.

I. ANSWER THE QUESTIONS

(Use the same words in the answers.)

1. Do you like to go to the movies?
2. When are we going to the mall?
3. Do you know where Joan is?
4. Was that very hard to do?
5. Is chocolate your favorite flavor?

HOW YOU DID

Spelling ________

	Super	Good	Getting Better	Needs Lots of Work
Punctuation				
Appearance				
Creativity				

LESSON 34

A. SPELL YOUR NEW WORDS

1. ______
2. ______
3. ______
4. ______
5. ______
6. ______

B. FILL IN THE BLANKS WITH YOUR SPELLING WORDS

1. I'm sorry I can't ______ your name.
2. Our ______ is changing. A new ______ moved in next door.
3. He ______ to play his drum very loudly.
4. My sister and I walked home ______ this evening.
5. We don't agree because we have ______ thoughts about the plan.

C. WHICH IS RIGHT?

find finds
finding found

They were ______ out what the problem was.

I hope they ______ it soon.

When they ______ out it was too late.

She always ______ the things I lose.

D. SENTENCE DICTATION

1. ______
2. ______
3. ______
4. ______
5. ______
6. ______
7. ______
8. ______
9. ______
10. ______

E. PROBLEM WORDS

1. ______
2. ______
3. ______
4. ______
5. ______

F. FILL IN THE BLANKS WITH YOUR SPELLING WORDS

I'm really lucky. My best friend is my next door __________ . We've grown up in this ______________ since we were very small. I ____________ when we had our first big adventure and got lost, and when we first _________ to go to school. And I remember how terrible it was when they put us in ____________ classes. It seemed like the worst thing in the world. But now that we are older we think it's better for learning when best friends aren't __________ in the same class.

G. MAKING SENTENCES

1. remember, went, together

1. ______________________________

2. began, different, way

2. ______________________________

H. MY OWN WRITING

Tell what you would change in the world if you could.

I. ANSWER THE QUESTIONS

(Use the same words in the answers.)

1. Do you know when she is coming?
2. What are they doing tomorrow?
3. Why haven't you done this yet?
4. How are you going to the mall?
5. Where did they put the new books?

HOW YOU DID

Spelling ______

	Super	Good	Getting Better	Needs Lots of Work
Punctuation				
Appearance				
Creativity				

LESSON 35

A. SPELL YOUR NEW WORDS

1. ______________
2. ______________
3. ______________
4. ______________
5. ______________
6. ______________
7. ______________
8. ______________

B. FILL IN THE BLANKS WITH YOUR SPELLING WORDS

1. Your friend hit the ball right __________ the window.
2. Something very __________ happened to me today. I won a writing contest.
3. Will you __________ your house with bricks or wood?
4. We __________ the strongest fence we could.
5. I __________ this puppy home __________ for you.

C. WHICH IS RIGHT?

carry carries
carrying carried

Can I help you __________ that?

He __________ my books when we walk together.

I __________ them so far my arms hurt.

Why aren't you __________ that for her?

D. SENTENCE DICTATION

____

1. ______________________________

____

2. ______________________________

____

3. ______________________________

____

4. ______________________________

____

5. ______________________________

____

6. ______________________________

____

7. ______________________________

____

8. ______________________________

____

9. ______________________________

____

10. ______________________________

____

E. PROBLEM WORDS

1. ______________
2. ______________
3. ______________
4. ______________
5. ______________

F. FILL IN THE BLANKS WITH YOUR SPELLING WORDS

In the corner of my yard there are some big bushes. I ________ some wood out there and I'm going to ________ myself a ________ place where I can go when I want to be alone. Sometimes I can get ________ the day without any problems. But there are some days when everybody is home or when the TV and radio are too noisy. Then I wish I had someplace to go, ________ when all this is going on at once and I need some peace. Just thinking about it sounds so great, I wish I had ________ it already.

G. MAKING SENTENCES

1. special / place / built

1. ____________________

2. noisy / especially / when

2. ____________________

H. MY OWN WRITING

What would you wish for if you really could have three wishes?

I. ANSWER THE QUESTIONS

(Use the same words in the answers.)

1. Are you going to the movies tonight?
2. When will dinner be ready?
3. Is your family coming to our house?
4. Where shall we go for our picnic?
5. Do you think he got hurt?

HOW YOU DID

Spelling ________

	Super	Good	Getting Better	Needs Lots of Work
Punctuation				
Appearance				
Creativity				

LESSON 36

A. SPELL YOUR NEW WORDS

1. ______
2. ______
3. ______
4. ______
5. ______
6. ______
7. ______
8. ______

B. FILL IN THE BLANKS WITH YOUR SPELLING WORDS

1. Do you ______ about ______ creatures?
2. We ______ go to school by bus.
3. I don't think it's ______ that there is life on the moon.
4. It's ______ to ______ what the world will be like in the year 3000.
5. It is the ______ thing to have hot days in summer and quite ______ for it to be cold.

C. PUT YOUR SPELLING WORDS IN ABC ORDER

1. ______
2. ______
3. ______
4. ______
5. ______
6. ______
7. ______
8. ______

D. SENTENCE DICTATION

1. ______
2. ______
3. ______
4. ______
5. ______
6. ______
7. ______
8. ______
9. ______
10. ______

E. PROBLEM WORDS

1. ______
2. ______
3. ______
4. ______
5. ______

F.

FILL IN THE BLANKS WITH YOUR SPELLING WORDS

Dreams can be so __________. The most __________ things can happen — things you couldn't even __________ while you're awake. It is the __________ thing to dream about people you know. But sometimes a __________ can be very frightening. Dreams are hard to understand. __________ you dream about things that seem __________ in real life. People have different ideas about what dreams mean. I think dreams are so interesting that it's just __________ that one day I'll be a scientist and study about dreams and the human mind.

G.

MAKING SENTENCES

1. strange / dreams / usually

1. ____

2. impossible / imagine / earth

2. ____

H.

MY OWN WRITING

Describe a frightening dream you had. Try to explain it.

____

I.

WHICH ONE SHOULD YOU USE?

usual usually unusual

1. The __________ thing for me to do after school is to take a bike ride.
2. It is __________ for us to go to the beach. We hardly ever go.
3. What do you __________ do in the evening?
4. That is a very __________ animal. It doesn't look like anything I ever saw.
5. I __________ do my homework right after school.

HOW YOU DID

Spelling __________

Super	Good	Getting Better	Needs Lots of Work

Punctuation

Appearance

Creativity

CUMULATIVE WORD LIST, VOLUME II

1. park town mall market movie (movies)
2. look help ride last show (looking) (helping) (marketing)
3. father children came learn teach (teacher) (friendly)
4. city country ball radio toy (toys) (showing)
5. took well today near far (taking)
6. man woman boy girl baby (men) (women)
7. drink fall draw picture sleep (sleepy) (asleep)
8. fast both back since paper (himself) (herself)
9. yet please once early late (later) (tried) (trying)
10. most next been hard happy (unhappy)
11. old also almost forget forgot (learned)
12. eat ate hold full call (called)
13. hurt while nothing clean dirt (dirty)
14. keep found such better cry (cries) (cried) (crying)
15. month year nice trouble color (colored)
16. few knew head life world (hardly)
17. shall grow afraid until ready (already)
18. family place around open close (opened) (closed)
19. word part left pretty walk (walked) (walking) (party)
20. hot cold bring small talk (talked) (talking)
21. still funny yesterday tomorrow laugh (laughed) (laughing)
22. stop watch else believe care (careful) (careless)
23. whole instead wonder start change (changed) (changing)
24. side thank move real really (inside) (outside) (beside)
25. hear heard light often happen (happened)
26. push pull carry none long (along) (countries)
27. wait alone thought piece slow (slowly)
28. high low fly stay water (we'll) (you'll)
29. sure street busy though decide (decided)
30. mean meant under guess finish (finished)
31. bought brought morning answer warm (warmer)
32. agree against being during hope (hoped) (hoping) (disagree)
33. begin between earth second noise (noisy) (beginning)
34. began together remember different neighbor (neighborhood)
35. build built through special especially (carries) (carried) (carrying)
36. dream imagine strange possible usual (usually) (unusual) (impossible)

TAKE HOME LESSON 36

(Make up sentences of your own using the remaining words.)

dream
imagine
strange
possible
usual
(usually)
(unusual)
(impossible)

1. I,don't think it's __________ for that __________ story to be true.

TAKE HOME LESSON 35

(Make up sentences of your own using the remaining words.)

build especially
built (carries)
through (carried)
special (carrying)

1. Did you __________ that house __________ for the new puppy?

TAKE HOME LESSON 34

(Make up sentences of your own using the remaining words.)

began
together
remember
different
(neighbor)
(neighborhood)

1. Our new __________ doesn't keep his yard clean and it spoils the __________.

TAKE HOME LESSON 33

(Make up sentences of your own using the remaining words.)

begin
between
earth
second
noise
(noisy)
(beginning)

1. Some say that in the __________ the __________ was a big ball of fire.

TAKE HOME LESSON 32

(Make up sentences of your own using the remaining words.)

agree hope
against (hoped)
being (hoping)
during (disagree)

1. We were __________ your team would play __________ ours.

TAKE HOME LESSON 31

(Make up sentences of your own using the remaining words.)

bought
brought
morning
answer
warm
(warmer)

1. It was much __________ when I woke up this __________.

TAKE HOME LESSON 36

Cut Along Dotted Line

TAKE HOME LESSON 35

Cut Along Dotted Line

TAKE HOME LESSON 34

Cut Along Dotted Line

TAKE HOME LESSON 33

Cut Along Dotted Line

TAKE HOME LESSON 32

Cut Along Dotted Line

TAKE HOME LESSON 31

TAKE HOME LESSON 30

(Make up sentences of your own using the remaining words.)

mean
meant
under
guess
finish
(finished)

1. I ________ to put all the shoes ________ the bed.

TAKE HOME LESSON 29

(Make up sentences of your own using the remaining words.)

sure
street
busy
though
decide
(decided)

1. I'm ________ he's too ________ to listen to me now.

TAKE HOME LESSON 28

(Make up sentences of your own using the remaining words.)

high
low
fly
stay
water
(we'll)
(you'll)

1. We'll ________ with you as long as ________ need us.

TAKE HOME LESSON 27

(Make up sentences of your own using the remaining words.)

wait
alone
thought
piece
slow
(slowly)

1. As I walked ________ down the country road I ________ about how beautiful it was.

TAKE HOME LESSON 26

(Make up sentences of your own using the remaining words.)

push
pull
carry
none
long
(along)
(countries)

1. Some ________ have many mountains and some have ________.

TAKE HOME LESSON 30

Cut Along Dotted Line

TAKE HOME LESSON 29

Cut Along Dotted Line

TAKE HOME LESSON 28

Cut Along Dotted Line

TAKE HOME LESSON 27

Cut Along Dotted Line

TAKE HOME LESSON 26

TAKE HOME LESSON 25

(Make up sentences of your own using the remaining words.)

hear
heard
light
often
happen
(happened)

1. I didn't ________ what ________ to Al. I know he had some trouble.

____

____

____

____

TAKE HOME LESSON 24

(Make up sentences of your own using the remaining words.)

side
thank
move
real
really
(inside)
(outside)
(beside)

1. If you want to sit ________ me I'll ________ over and make room.

____

____

____

____

TAKE HOME LESSON 23

(Make up sentences of your own using the remaining words.)

whole
start
wonder
instead
change
(changed)
(changing)

1. Please don't ________ your mind again.

____

____

____

____

TAKE HOME LESSON 22

(Make up sentences of your own using the remaining words.)

stop
watch
else
believe
care
(careful)
(careless)

1. You must ________ being so ________ with your work.

____

____

____

____

TAKE HOME LESSON 21

(Make up sentences of your own using the remaining words.)

still
funny
yesterday
tomorrow
laugh
(laughed)
(laughing)

1. I ________ so hard at the show ________ that my stomach hurt.

____

____

____

____

TAKE HOME LESSON 25

Cut Along Dotted Line

TAKE HOME LESSON 24

Cut Along Dotted Line

TAKE HOME LESSON 23

Cut Along Dotted Line

TAKE HOME LESSON 22

Cut Along Dotted Line

TAKE HOME LESSON 21

TAKE HOME LESSON 20

(Make up sentences of your own using the remaining words.)

hot
cold
bring
small
talk
(talked)
(talking)

1. Let's bring some ________ food and some ________ drinks to the party.

TAKE HOME LESSON 19

(Make up sentences of your own using the remaining words.)

word
part
left
pretty
walk
(walked)
(walking)
(party)

1. I ________ right by that ________ girl without saying one word.

TAKE HOME LESSON 18

(Make up sentences of your own using the remaining words.)

family
place
around
open
close
(opened)
(closed)

1. Let's go ________ the corner and look for a ________ that's open.

TAKE HOME LESSON 17

(Make up sentences of your own using the remaining words.)

shall
grow
afraid
until
ready
(already)

1. What ________ we do ________ they come?

TAKE HOME LESSON 16

(Make up sentences of your own using the remaining words.)

few
knew
head
life
world
(hardly)

1. Turn down that road and let's ________ for the lake.

TAKE HOME LESSON 20

Cut Along Dotted Line

TAKE HOME LESSON 19

Cut Along Dotted Line

TAKE HOME LESSON 18

Cut Along Dotted Line

TAKE HOME LESSON 17

Cut Along Dotted Line

TAKE HOME LESSON 16

TAKE HOME LESSON 15

(Make up sentences of your own using the remaining words.)

month
year
nice
trouble
color
(colored)

1. The ________ you chose for your room is very ________ .

TAKE HOME LESSON 14

(Make up sentences of your own using the remaining words.)

keep
found
such
better
cry
(cries)
(cried)
(crying)

1. Don't ______ . I'm sure things will get ________ .

TAKE HOME LESSON 13

(Make up sentences of your own using the remaining words.)

hurt
while
nothing
clean
dirt
(dirty)

1. This place is so ________ we had better ________ it up.

TAKE HOME LESSON 12

(Make up sentences of your own using the remaining words.)

eat
ate
hold
full
call
(called)

1. I am going to ________ you to ______ lunch with me tomorrow.

TAKE HOME LESSON 11

(Make up sentences of your own using the remaining words.)

old
also
almost
forget
forgot
(learned)

1. I already ________ what we ________ in class last week.

TAKE HOME LESSON 15

Cut Along Dotted Line

TAKE HOME LESSON 14

Cut Along Dotted Line

TAKE HOME LESSON 13

Cut Along Dotted Line

TAKE HOME LESSON 10

Cut Along Dotted Line

TAKE HOME LESSON 11

TAKE HOME LESSON 10

(Make up sentences of your own using the remaining words.)

most
next
been
hard
happy
(unhappy)

1. It makes me __________ to see them work so ________.

____

____

____

____

TAKE HOME LESSON 9

(Make up sentences of your own using the remaining words.)

yet
please
once
early
late
(later)
(tried)
(trying)

1. Just this ________ will you please come home ________.

____

____

____

____

TAKE HOME LESSON 8

(Make up sentences of your own using the remaining words.)

fast
both
back
since
paper
(himself)
(herself)

1. She completed the work on the school ________ all by __________.

____

____

____

____

TAKE HOME LESSON 7

(Make up sentences of your own using the remaining words.)

drink
fall
draw
picture
sleep
(sleepy)
(asleep)

1. I'm so __________ I can't stay up another minute.

____

____

____

____

TAKE HOME LESSON 6

(Make up sentences of your own using the remaining words.)

man
woman
boy
girl
baby
(men)
(women)

1. That ________ and __________ are friends of my parents.

____

____

____

____

TAKE HOME LESSON 10

Cut Along Dotted Line

TAKE HOME LESSON 9

Cut Along Dotted Line

TAKE HOME LESSON 8

Cut Along Dotted Line

TAKE HOME LESSON 7

Cut Along Dotted Line

TAKE HOME LESSON 6

TAKE HOME LESSON 5

(Make up sentences of your own using the remaining words.)

took
well
today
near
far
(taking)

1. What will you be ________ to the picnic?

____
____
____
____

TAKE HOME LESSON 4

(Make up sentences of your own using the remaining words.)

city
country
ball
radio
toy
(toys)
(showing)

1. I was ____________ them all the pictures I painted.

____
____
____
____

TAKE HOME LESSON 3

(Make up sentences of your own using the remaining words.)

father
children
came
learn
teach
(teacher)
(friendly)

1. How many ____________ are there in your family?
2. Are those new people next door ____________?
3. My __________ and his family __________ from another country.

____
____

TAKE HOME LESSON 2

(Make up sentences of your own using the remaining words.)

look
help
ride
last
show
(looking)
(helping)
(marketing)

________ night we were ____________ at a __________ on TV. It was about how we could help older men and women. Some people ________ with the ____________ . Some will give them a ________ downtown. The program said that sometimes you can just be company for them and ________ at TV shows together or read to them if their eyes are bad. I think ____________ people can make you feel good.

TAKE HOME LESSON 1

(Make up sentences of your own using the remaining words.)

park
town
mall
market
movie
(movies)

They just built a new ________ in our ________ . It has lots of nice shops, a __________ theater, a big food __________ , and even a small ________ in the middle with trees and flowers and places to sit. Last night my family all went there. We went to the ___________ and saw a good show. Then we got some fruit and cookies at the ___________ and had a snack on a bench in the park.

TAKE HOME LESSON 5

Cut Along Dotted Line

TAKE HOME LESSON 4

Cut Along Dotted Line

TAKE HOME LESSON 3

Cut Along Dotted Line

TAKE HOME LESSON 2

Cut Along Dotted Line

TAKE HOME LESSON 1

NOTES

NOTES

NOTES

NOTES

NOTES

NOTES